G000016687

HORSHAM
THEN & NOW
IN COLOUR

DAVID ARSCOTT

First published in 2011

The History Press
The Mill, Brimscombe Port
Stroud, Gloucestershire, GL5 2QG
www.thehistorypress.co.uk

British Library Cataloguing in Publication Data.
A catalogue record for this book is available from the British Library.

ISBN 978 0 7524 6346 9

Typesetting and origination by The History Press
Printed in India
Manufacturing managed by Jellyfish Print Solutions Ltd

CONTENTS

ACKNOWLEDGEMENTS

In a suspicious world the trust and kindness of postcard and photograph collectors shines like a beacon. Two in particular must be mentioned here, both moved by a love of Horsham and a remarkable spirit of generosity to lend me wonderful material for my book. John Cannon provided the bulk of the illustrations, and I can only hope that he feels I have done them something like justice. The late Cecil Cramp not only weighed in with many more, but entertained me with vivid, often humorous, memories of bygone Horsham for good measure. Where I am in error it will be despite their plentiful advice and information.

ABOUT THE AUTHOR

A former newspaper journalist and BBC producer and presenter, David Arscott is a freelance writer with some fifty titles to his name, many of them on Sussex themes. He founded the Sussex Book Club and runs Pomegranate Press, which specialises in taking authors of all kinds through the self-publishing process. The honorary secretary of the Society of Sussex Authors, he lives in Lewes with his wife and three children.

INTRODUCTION

Horsham is apt to mystify the motorised stranger, who is swept into the canyon of Albion Way, funnelled into a multi-storey car park and deposited in a teeming shopping mall among a warren of narrow streets. The abundance of brand spanking new multi-storey blocks alongside the wide main roads advertises the town's major remodelling in recent times.

The good news is that this bold makeover favours the pedestrian. Crossing the urban racetrack is not a pleasant experience, but most of the town can be walked well away from this hurly-burly. The head-scratching interloper will soon discover that the wholesale reconstruction of the fringing townscape has had the effect of preserving the essence of its historic centre. The locals seem to feel that this has been a price worth paying – and they ought to know best.

This is unashamedly a book about the heart of the town, where continuities and disruptions make for a fascinating tour. Part of the pleasure of picking a way through the criss-crossing thoroughfares is to come across a remembered building from a different angle, so that we eventually find ourselves thoroughly familiarised. (I speak as a non-native who has had to learn the geography step by step.) Nowhere are we more than half a mile from Carfax, the central hub, and in this small span we find the restless history of the town unfolding before us.

Horsham's founding fathers were Saxon colonisers of the Weald who drove their animals to pasture here during the spring and summer months. The settlement grew rapidly after the Norman conquest, with a substantial church, an assize court and the county gaol. During the sixteenth and seventeenth centuries the Weald was home to a highly profitable iron industry, and Horsham became a staging post for the coaching trade and the fulcrum of a range of rural industries including brickmaking, tanning and brewing.

The town housed the military during the Napoleonic Wars and was given a further boost by the coming of the railway in the 1840s. By the time that the older photographs in this book were taken it had all the accoutrements of a comfortable market town with substantial public buildings, small factories and well-stocked shops.

Horsham has been lucky both in its modern historians and in its avid collectors of old photographs and picture postcards. The generosity of the latter has made my task entirely pleasurable and has ensured a wealth of illustrations from which to choose. My own photographs, taken in March 2011, are certainly not intended as collectors' items, but I hope they at least help explain some elements of the streetscape which would otherwise be inscrutable.

Will another such book be required a generation from now? I rather hope not. No community can, or should, resist sensible change, but having just emerged in surprisingly good heart from a truly cataclysmic upheaval, Horsham has surely earned the right to take a deep breath and put its proverbial feet up.

CARFAX, WEST SIDE

IN THIS PHOTOGRAPH, taken in about 1906 (left), the Wesleyan Sunday school parades past Linton's wholesale grocery and provision works. Further to the right, with the semi-circular façade, are the offices of the *West Sussex Gazette* in a building which later became the Workers' Education Association Hall and, later still, the Women's Institute Market Hall.
(Reproduced with kind permission of Cecil Cramp)

THIS SIDE OF Carfax has undergone more drastic changes than the other three. Swan Walk, the town's only indoor shopping area, now stands behind the route of the parade in the old photograph, leaving not a trace behind. The Duke of Norfolk laid the mall's foundation stone in 1973. It opened three years later and now houses more than fifty stores.

CARFAX, NORTH SIDE

THE FORMER STOCKS and whipping post stood in the north-west corner of Carfax until the 1940s, when they were removed to the town museum. The photograph on the right is from about 1922 and shows the offices of King & Barnes brewery (the building with the arch) and the post office (its front covered with ivy).

(Reproduced with kind permission of John Cannon)

ONLY THE HOUSE on the left has survived modern changes. The brewery closed in 2000, after some 200 years in the town, although its last director, Bill King, swiftly launched a 'micro' brewery, W.J. King. The post office was demolished in 1973 but (as we can see) reopened only a hop away in one of the new blocks.

LOOKING NORTH FROM CARFAX

THE BANDSTAND WAS erected in 1891 and the tree was planted in the same year, which dates the old photograph on the right to the early years of the twentieth century. The fountain in the foreground was installed in 1897 to mark Queen Victoria's diamond jubilee.

(Reproduced with kind permission of John Cannon)

THERE'S A GOOD deal of continuity in the modern picture, although the jubilee fountain had to make way for traffic in 1977 (it was re-erected in Copnall Way). Keep walking and you'll discover that the spired tower of St Mark's church on the right now stands alone. The rest of the redundant building was pulled down to accommodate the town centre redevelopment scheme in 1989, making way for the Royal & Sun Alliance headquarters.

11

CARFAX, EAST SIDE

THE THEATRE ROYAL originally opened as the Electric Theatre in 1911, and you reached it via a narrow alleyway to the right of the Stout House. Six years later the owners bought the shop on the other side of the pub, giving themselves the attractive new entrance that can still be seen in this photograph. The war memorial on the right of the picture was unveiled on Armistice Day 1921. *(Reproduced with kind permission of John Cannon)*

THE THEATRE ON the left edge of picture, has long since gone but the Stout House remains – and still has its proud King & Barnes frontage, despite the brewery's demise. The war memorial was moved to the north side of Carfax in 1992, when the names of Second World War casualties were added. A surprising difference between the old and new pictures is the decline in traffic: buses stop here and lorries unload but most cars have been re-routed elsewhere.

13

PIRIES PLACE

THE CENTRAL MARKET, east of Carfax, in 1951
(left). Piries Place was a row of fifteen Victorian
cottages built by the headmaster of Collyer's
School, William Piries, and – he was a Scot –
decorated with a thistle design.
(Reproduced with kind permission of John Cannon)

AND HERE IS Mr Piries, on the right, in the
donkey cart he habitually drove around the town.
The bronze sculpture, designed by Lorne McKean,
sits in the iron and glass shopping precinct which
replaced the earlier development in 1989.

15

CARFAX, SOUTH-EAST SIDE

IN 1877 THE Duke of Norfolk referred to the large central area of Carfax as 'all that waste and unenclosed land', and the photograph below shows that things weren't very different at the beginning of the twentieth century.
(Reproduced with kind permission of Cecil Cramp)

IT'S A MUCH more lived-in space today, with a broad pedestrianised area flanked by a taxi rank, which can be seen on the right of the picture. The architecture is very little changed, and the lamp standards (rather more of them than in the past) match the elegance of their decidedly taller predecessors – a feature of old Horsham.

THE CROWN INN, CARFAX

'GOOD ACCOMMODATION FOR cyclists' proclaims the sign by the Crown Inn door in this photograph of 1906 (left). It has occupied this site since 1805 and actually comprises four separate buildings. Note a fine example of one of those ornate old Horsham lamp standards.
(Reproduced with kind permission of John Cannon)

THE CROWN HAS had a refit in recent times and is now more of a restaurant than a down-to-earth town pub. The minimalist hanging sign tastefully matches the restrained green tinge of the paintwork.

THE KING'S HEAD HOTEL, CARFAX

THE FAÇADE OF Horsham's only town-centre hotel was fashioned during the eighteenth century, but the date 1401 on the wall may be an accurate guide to the age of the earliest parts of the building.

In this photograph of 1907 (left) a German prince is seen arriving at the hotel with the first military Rolls Royces. The Inland Revenue had its offices here from 1855 until 1881 – one of its officers being a Mr Thrift.
(Reproduced with kind permission of John Cannon)

THE SIGNAGE REMAINS but the hotel closed in 2004 and still awaits redevelopment. Planning permission has been granted for the former forty-two bedrooms to be reduced to seventeen, with the freed space being given over to shops, restaurants and offices. The Horsham Society has described the boarded-up building as 'a blight on the townscape' and has urged the council to buy it and retain its outward appearance.

MIDDLE STREET/
SOUTH STREET

THE CAREFULLY POSED photograph below from the 1920s shows the staff of the local grocer and wine merchant impeccably turned out. Churchman took in its goods at both first- and

second-floor level, which explains the gantry and the fold-down platforms beneath the windows. The owner and his family lived above the premises in the house on the left. *(Reproduced with kind permission of John Cannon)*

PERHAPS THANKS TO the building's Grade II listing which was awarded in 1949, the hoist and fold-down platforms remain, but the fabric needs a little tender loving care at first-floor level. Poor Martha has been denied her apostrophe above the furniture store next door – perhaps intentionally in a more shoulder-shrugging grammatical age.

MIDDLE STREET/ CARFAX

MIDDLE STREET, AT the junction with Carfax. By 1951, when this photograph was taken, Middle Street was already pedestrianised, although traffic could (as the sign shows) sweep past on its way to Guildford, Dorking and London. The building on the extreme left of the

picture was the Chart and Lawrence department store. Mr Camplin the chemist, opposite, had his own dark room for developing and printing films.
(Reproduced with kind permission of John Cannon)

ON THE LEFT we see one of the worst of Horsham's modern developments, with uncompromising brick blocks facing one another at each corner and a hideous replacement (occupied by the Non Stop Party Shop) for the half-timbered building in the older picture.

THE TOWN HALL

THIS IS A building in two parts. The old market house on the site had been used for the assizes and when it was converted into a town hall in 1812 space was set aside for court rooms on each floor. In 1888 it was completely rebuilt except for the north front (seen here) with the arms of the Crown, Horsham and the Dukes of Norfolk. The postcard of 1905 is unusual in that it advertises the Temperance Hotel founded by Jury Cramp, the owner of a jeweller's shop which moved from Market Square via Middle Street to West Street. The hotel struggled on for about eight years but virtue was obliged to be its only reward. 'It's an excellent way to lose money' Mr Cramp would say.

(Reproduced with kind permission of Cecil Cramp)

THE BLANKNESS OF the area in front of the town hall may eventually be improved, since the council announced in 2007 (these things take time) that 'the relationship between the town hall and nearby Market Square and East Street is... being looked at, so that this part of the town can potentially work better together'. The Bear Inn, having long seen off Jury Cramp's Temperance Hotel, now has a reputation for serving a good range of real ales.

27

THE CAUSEWAY

THIS IS PROBABLY the most photographed street in Lewes.
E.V. Lucas, in his *Highways and Byways of Sussex* (1904),
declared that: 'there is in England no more peaceful and
prosperous row of venerable homes than the Causeway,
joining Carfax and the church, with its pollarded limes and
chestnuts in line on the pavement's edge, its graceful gables,
jutting eaves and glimpses of green gardens through the doors
and windows. The sweetest part of Horsham is there.'
(Reproduced with kind permission of John Cannon)

THE TREES IN the postcard of 1903 eventually came to
the end of their natural span, and the replacements we see
were planted in 1940. Horsham Museum has been housed
here since 1941 and (along with this book, of course) is
a good starting point for any exploration of Horsham. In
July 2008 the Causeway became a film set for *31 North 62
East*, a psychological thriller starring Marina Sirtis about an
SAS veteran who seeks justice after being betrayed by the
government.

THE CAUSEWAY AND CHURCH

THE HOUSE IN the foreground of this *c.* 1910 picture is a typical Horsham hall-house with two cross-wings, each of which is jettied at the front: it projects above the street. Next to it is a house covered with ivy, a popular adornment at the time.
(Reproduced with kind permission of John Cannon)

THE TWO HOUSES have now become one, known as Minstrels, and the removal of the ivy and additions to the façade of the lower part reveal that it was originally a continuous jetty house.

ST MARY'S CHURCH

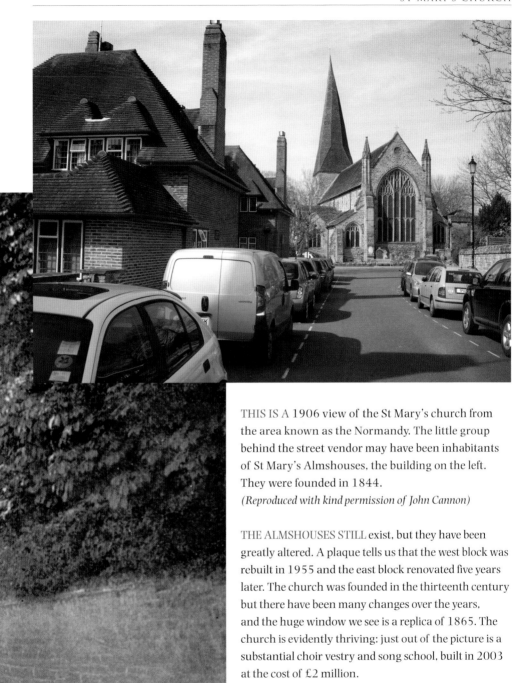

THIS IS A 1906 view of the St Mary's church from the area known as the Normandy. The little group behind the street vendor may have been inhabitants of St Mary's Almshouses, the building on the left. They were founded in 1844.
(Reproduced with kind permission of John Cannon)

THE ALMSHOUSES STILL exist, but they have been greatly altered. A plaque tells us that the west block was rebuilt in 1955 and the east block renovated five years later. The church was founded in the thirteenth century but there have been many changes over the years, and the huge window we see is a replica of 1865. The church is evidently thriving: just out of the picture is a substantial choir vestry and song school, built in 2003 at the cost of £2 million.

THE FORMER COLLYER'S SCHOOL

COLLYER'S SCHOOL IS today in Hurst Road off North Street but it was in this building off Denne Road from 1840 until 1892. Once the boys had gone, Denne Road Girls' School moved in, staying here until it was demolished in the 1960s.

(Reproduced with kind permission of John Cannon)

SIC TRANSIT GLORIA. This playground (left), with St Mary's primary school behind, is the site of the former Collyer's School. It would have been good to picture children at their play but a photographer risks arrest for taking such shots today.

THE OLD
TOWN MILL

WE KNOW THAT there was a mill in Horsham
before 1231, and it can't have been far from here,
using the waters of the Arun. This is the old town
mill in a photograph of 1906 (right). The water
was deeper in the early twentieth century than it
is now and when Collyer's School was close by the
church, the boys would swim here.
(Reproduced with kind permission of John Cannon)

PROVENDER MI

THE MILL HAS had a chequered modern history but it was rescued from collapse by a conversion into offices in 1990. (The date is recorded in roman numerals on a sundial.) Since then it has had periods of standing empty, but its future seems secure whether for business or residential use.

DENNE ROAD

WHEN IT WAS the major north-south route through Horsham, Denne Road was described as a 'great highway from Southwater to the heath'. By the time this photograph was taken around 1909 it was a backwater, albeit lying close to the town centre, and these children were virtually in the countryside. *(Reproduced with kind permission of John Cannon)*

IT'S NOT MUCH busier today, although the road markings show that cars come this way. Note the 'no through road' sign on the railway bridge. There are houses beyond but the road eventually peters out.

WEST STREET/ SOUTH STREET

THE CORNER OF West Street and South Street, seen from Middle Street. This photograph (right) was taken in about 1929 with the Timothy Whites sign prominent on the north side where a long overhang of blinds protects shoppers from the glare. The traffic system is evidently one-way since all the cars and neatly parked bicycles are facing east towards Middle Street.
(Reproduced with kind permission of John Cannon)

THE ROAD IS completely pedestrianised today. The architecture on the left is largely unchanged but the buildings with the blinds in the foreground have gone.

J.H. SAYERS, WEST STREET

THE HORSHAM PICTORIAL Trade Record of August 1912, about the time this advertising card was produced, reported that 'Mr Sayers invariably shows a fine stock of the best classes of fresh water and sea fish according to season, including salmon, lobsters, crabs, oysters etc. The day's supply is on hand by eight o'clock each morning, and the buying at Billingsgate is

Telegrams—"Sayers, Horsham."   Telephone 11 P.O. Horsham.

Agent for Shippam's

AND CAMBRIDG

J. H

Fish,

Poult

LONDON HOUS

55 West

Nearly opposit

Agent for Overall Cod Liver Oil.

conducted under the personal supervision of Mr Sayers, whose business also embraces poultry in season and, as a licensed dealer in game, rabbits, hares, pheasants, pigeons, and partridges and wild fowl are dealt in both wholesale and retail.'
(Reproduced with kind permission of John Cannon)

THE STREET NUMBERS have changed slightly, but the windows in the photograph above reveal that this is the Sayers emporium in its somewhat less appealing modern guise.

ALBERY'S, WEST STREET

THIS SADDLER'S BUSINESS was run by the Horsham historian William Albery when this picture (opposite) was taken early in the twentieth century. He was also a noted calligrapher and a champion bugle player.
(Reproduced with kind permission of John Cannon)

ALBERY, DESPITE HIS many community interests, was a notoriously shy man who hated having his photograph taken. Fortunately the staff of the family-run jewellery chain that now occupies his former premises are less self-effacing. Our picture shows store manager Dominic Toomey (right) and assistant manager Anton Iebba.

Saddler and Harness Maker,

(Certificated by the London Saddlers' Company),

Portmanteaux & Leather Cases

Made and Repaired on the Premises.

Established by Geo. Albery, 1810.

49 ALBERY. 49

W. ALBERY

SADDLER HARNESS & ROPEMAKER

Series by the Scottish Photographic Touring and Pictorial Post Ca

WEST ST., HOR

WEST STREET, LOOKING EAST FROM THE SWAN

INNS WEREN'T ONLY for drinking in days gone by, and the Swan was a staging post for horse-drawn coaches as well as being used as a corn market in the late eighteenth century and

a poultry market a hundred years later. One local who did use it for the obvious purpose was Bysshe Shelley, grandfather of the poet, who enjoyed animated conversations at the Swan before rolling back to his home in Denne Road. Our photograph of 1885 (left) also shows the Castle Inn in the middle distance.
(Reproduced with kind permission of John Cannon)

MUCH OF THE architecture is unchanged, but the Swan disappeared in the 1970s to make way for the Swan Walk development. Shopping malls can bring about the demise of small traders in the vicinity, but West Street remains busy despite the nearby competition of Swan Walk.

WEST STREET, WEST END

THIS IS THE south side of the street, near Bishopric in 1951. As the position of the parked car suggests, there was a one-way system in place at this time, with traffic heading towards the Carfax.
(Reproduced with kind permission of Cecil Cramp)

SOME OF THE buildings remain but Dixeys, the optician's, seems to be the only constant in trading terms. Trading in this area goes back centuries. In 1449 Henry VI granted a charter for the holding of a market each Monday in 'le Westrete'– which became the poultry market.

WEST STREET
FROM
BISHOPRIC

THE BLACK HORSE, on the far corner, was
fondly known to locals as 'the old kicker'. At one
time, like the Swan, it had been used to trade
grain but in 1868 a pillared Italianate corn
exchange with a market hall and assembly room
was built next door to it. The photograph dates
from 1951.
(Reproduced with kind permission of John Cannon)

THIS END OF Bishopric has become Bishopric Square and has heavy new buildings all around. The Black Horse, the corn exchange and the building on the left of the old picture have given way to ugly modern developments, while a McDonald's now occupies the site of the Gilbert Rice showroom. The large, globe-shaped fountain or 'water sculpture' of 1996 (aka The Rising Universe) commemorates the poet Percy Bysshe Shelley, who lived locally but was disowned by his father because of his atheistic and revolutionary views. The fountain has been controversial, and when it fell into disrepair *West Sussex County Times* readers voted to have it removed – but the council decided to keep it, and the water is now gushing again.

BISHOPRIC, LOOKING EAST

THE BROAD EXPANSE of Bishopric was wide enough to have cattle pens erected on each side, and the livestock market was held here until 1913, when traffic became too heavy

for comfort. This view dates from around 1955. Henry Burstow, the shoemaker and bell-ringer whose *Reminiscences of Horsham* describes life in the town during the Victorian era, was born in one of the cottages beyond the Kings Arms in 1828.
(Reproduced with kind permission of John Cannon)

ALAS FOR THE ghost of Henry Burstow: the Kings Arms remains, but his cottage has gone. Bishopric now feeds traffic into Albion Way, which sweeps around the centre of the town.

BISHOPRIC/ SPRINGFIELD ROAD

THIS IMPOSING BUILDING, erected in 1899 on land owned by the Roman Catholic Church, was occupied by Seagrave's bakery when this picture (right) was taken in 1907. The delicious smell of new-baked bread rising from the cellars remains a fond memory for older Horsham residents.
(Reproduced with kind permission of Cecil Cramp)

NOW PART OF Bishopric Square, this uncompromising block (left) stands on the Seagraves site. During the early fifteenth century the crossroads here was known as Lynd Cross – and that's the name given to the modern pub.

THE RAILWAY STATION

THE VERY FIRST station was built in 1848 (at the end of a single-track branch line from Three Bridges, Crawley) but this is the replacement of 1859 when horse-drawn buses ran to and from the King's Head Hotel in Carfax. Various improvements were made to the rail service in the early years and a new route to Dorking, Leatherhead and London opened in 1867. *(Reproduced with kind permission of John Cannon)*

THE PRESENT GRADE II listed station was built by the Southern Railway in the International Modern

style in 1938 to coincide with the electrification of the line. Ian Nairn, in the Sussex volume of the 'Buildings of England' series, describes the front as 'really horrible', which is perhaps a little unkind. It is on both the Arun Valley Line 38 miles (61km) south of London Victoria and the Sutton & Mole Valley Line, which terminates at Horsham.

THE STATION HOTEL

CAR HIRE WAS one of the services offered by the hotel back in 1910 when this photograph was taken. The siting of early railway stations often aroused great controversy and the hotel originally earmarked for the station, the Pioneer, eventually found itself too far away from the chosen spot to pick up any railway business. The building itself still stands in Elm Grove off Brighton Road. *(Reproduced with kind permission of John Cannon)*

THE BUILDING IS now owned by the countrywide Beefeater chain of pubs and restaurants, and the word 'hotel' has disappeared from the title (there's a 64-bedroom Premier Inn next door though). The telephone number in the meantime has changed from 'Horsham 16' to eleven digits.

NORTH STREET SHOP

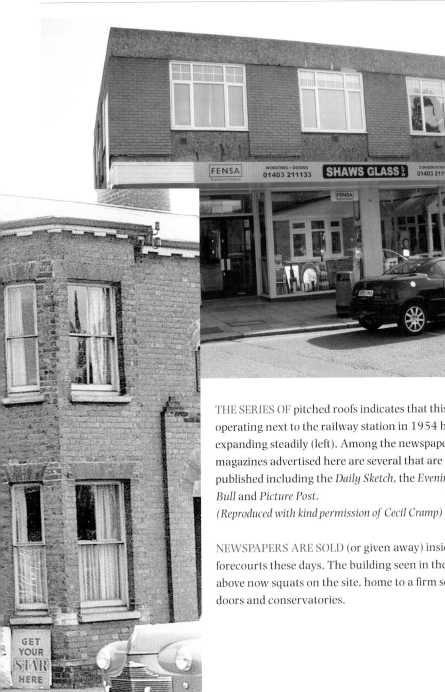

THE SERIES OF pitched roofs indicates that this business operating next to the railway station in 1954 had been expanding steadily (left). Among the newspapers and magazines advertised here are several that are no longer published including the *Daily Sketch*, the *Evening News*, *John Bull* and *Picture Post*.
(Reproduced with kind permission of Cecil Cramp)

NEWSPAPERS ARE SOLD (or given away) inside station forecourts these days. The building seen in the photograph above now squats on the site, home to a firm selling windows, doors and conservatories.

NORTH STREET, TOWARDS THE STATION

UNTIL THE MARKET was moved from Bishopric to the station goods yard, cattle and other animals had to be driven between the two sites every Wednesday. In the old photograph (left) of around 1912 the former double-fronted station building can be seen in the distance.
(Reproduced with kind permission of John Cannon)

THE LAYOUT HASN'T changed but a pedestrian would be more than a little startled to be confronted by a herd of cows today. The entrance to Horsham Park is off to the left.

NORTH CHAPEL,
NORTH STREET

IN 1457 A guild and chantry was based at the altar of St John the Baptist on the south side of the parish church, and when chantries were abolished under Henry VIII a hundred years later the 'brotherhood' responsible for it were said to own a house 'lying in the North street, with the kitchen, stable and garden'. This venerable building, long known as North Chapel, is believed to be that very house, albeit with later additions.

(Reproduced with kind permission of John Cannon)

SO DRASTIC HAVE been the changes in North Street between the station and the town centre that it's surprising to find this handsome survivor (left). It now serves as offices for the PMMS consultancy group. Across the road, near the entrance to Horsham Park, is a cluster of other old buildings which the developers have spared.

NORTH STREET, WEST SIDE

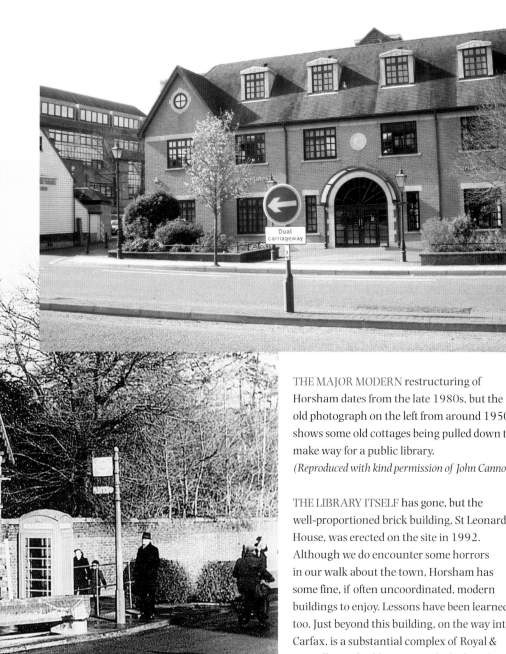

THE MAJOR MODERN restructuring of Horsham dates from the late 1980s, but the old photograph on the left from around 1950 shows some old cottages being pulled down to make way for a public library.
(Reproduced with kind permission of John Cannon)

THE LIBRARY ITSELF has gone, but the well-proportioned brick building, St Leonards House, was erected on the site in 1992. Although we do encounter some horrors in our walk about the town, Horsham has some fine, if often uncoordinated, modern buildings to enjoy. Lessons have been learned too. Just beyond this building, on the way into Carfax, is a substantial complex of Royal & Sun Alliance buildings, one of which replaced a much-loathed ten-storey tower block called Stocklund House, demolished in 1992.

NORTH STREET/
PARK STREET

THE CHURCH HELPS us fix our bearings in this 1903 scene littered with advertising signs. The
timber-framed building on the left is Perry Place, with Park Street forking left off North Street

beyond it. The building in the centre of the picture, where the two roads meet, houses Chart's Corn Stores – run by a Horsham character, Amos Chart.
(Reproduced with kind permission of John Cannon)

THE IMPRESSIVE MODERN blocks on the east side of North Street have erased all memories of former buildings – although Perry Place itself was dismantled and removed to Mannings Heath as early as 1912. It stood close to the spot from which this photograph was taken, on the site now occupied by the Heath Lambert insurance company. Amos Chart's building survives (its white wall faces us) as do the cottages on the right of the picture – one of them the Black Jug pub. North Street now ends here, and you reach the church tower on foot along Chart Way.

EAST STREET FROM MIDDLE STREET

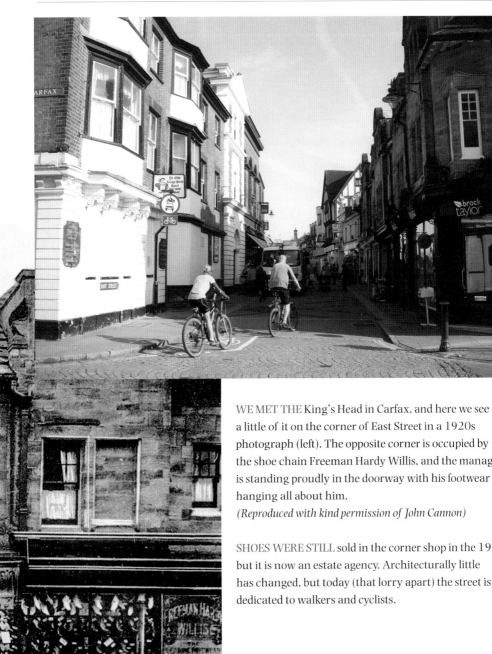

WE MET THE King's Head in Carfax, and here we see a little of it on the corner of East Street in a 1920s photograph (left). The opposite corner is occupied by the shoe chain Freeman Hardy Willis, and the manager is standing proudly in the doorway with his footwear hanging all about him.

(Reproduced with kind permission of John Cannon)

SHOES WERE STILL sold in the corner shop in the 1950s, but it is now an estate agency. Architecturally little has changed, but today (that lorry apart) the street is dedicated to walkers and cyclists.

71

EAST STREET, LOOKING EAST

THE PHOTOGRAPHER ATTRACTED quite a crowd when he snapped the street in 1904. The Anchor Hotel sign can be seen beyond the millinery shop on the right, with another for Horsham Working Men's Club. One of the town's elaborate lamp standards graces the street further along. *(Reproduced with kind permission of John Cannon)*

AMONG THE NUMERABLE changes in a little more than a century is the cupola above the corner building on the left of the picture. Shop blinds are no longer in fashion but the Strada restaurant still sports one. This photograph on the left was taken from a spot close to Anchor Court, a passageway whose name remembers the former inn.

EAST STREET,
LOOKING
WEST

DID THE SAME crowd-pulling photographer take this shot from Denne Road in 1906? The little girl at the front is on an errand with her milk churn. Although everyone has stopped for the camera, this scene reflects the bustling nature of what was one of the town's busiest streets, with many

workaday necessities catered for: china, weighing scales, newspapers, boots and shoes, dairy products and so on.
(Reproduced with kind permission of John Cannon)

THE STREET IS pedestrianised today, but passers-by have to negotiate quite an obstacle course in the way of advertisement boards, seats and shrubs in pots. Its character is different today, but it still retains a number of specialist shops. Twittens off the street lead to several mews hidden behind and East Street is the main access to the drill hall in Denne Road – a venue for a wide range of indoor events.

MEDIEVAL HALL-HOUSE, EAST STREET

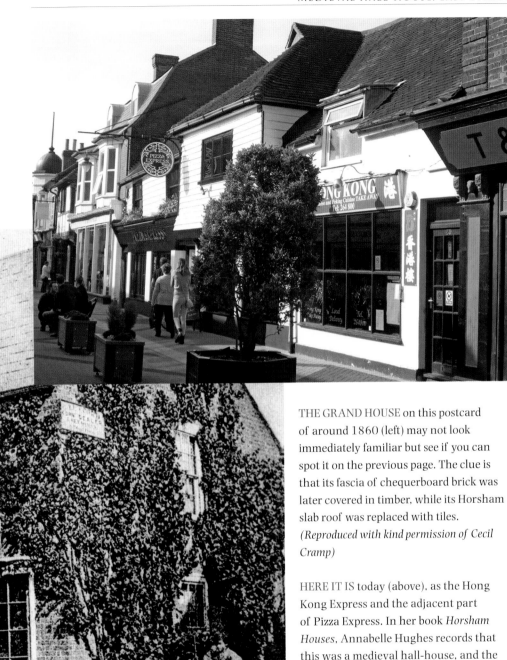

THE GRAND HOUSE on this postcard of around 1860 (left) may not look immediately familiar but see if you can spot it on the previous page. The clue is that its fascia of chequerboard brick was later covered in timber, while its Horsham slab roof was replaced with tiles. *(Reproduced with kind permission of Cecil Cramp)*

HERE IT IS today (above), as the Hong Kong Express and the adjacent part of Pizza Express. In her book *Horsham Houses*, Annabelle Hughes records that this was a medieval hall-house, and the projecting part was a jettied cross-wing with an upstairs window in the western end that looked up to Middle Street.

EAST STREET/DENNE ROAD

THE SPLENDID 1922 photograph on the left shows the newsagent's tempting passing customers with a wide range of billboard headlines, among them 'Taxi Murder Inquest Surprise', 'The Prime Minister's Speech' and 'Higher Prices Premier's Admission' – it was an election year, and Lloyd George's Liberals were soon to be ousted by Bonar Law's Conservatives, with Labour in second place.

(Reproduced with kind permission of John Cannon)

THE TONE IS much more subdued today, but a newsagent still occupies the corner site. Horsham has its own regional newspaper, the *West Sussex County Times*, which is based in the centre, at Market Square. It has bucked the trend by remaining a broadsheet.

EAST STREET/
BARTELLOT ROAD

IT'S 1951, AND the site long occupied by C. Brewer & Sons, the decorators' merchants, has been cleared for redevelopment (left). The advertisers have been quick to move in, their hoardings promoting Ovaltine, Bourn-vita, Oxo, Sanatogen Tonic Wine and a visit to the *Daily Mail*-sponsored Ideal Home Exhibition.
(Reproduced with kind permission of John Cannon)

IT'S IMPOSSIBLE to credit the architect of the pile which later arose on the site with an ounce of sensitivity or originality. This rebarbative fortress is now shared by Pets at Home and the Majestic Wine Warehouse. They are not to blame.

EAST STREET, EASTERN END

THE RAILWAY BRIDGE in the distance gives the perspective for this photograph of around 1900 (below). The two men on the far left are standing at the entrance to Bartellot Road. The bridge (locally always referred to as 'the Iron Bridge') isn't very far off the ground and several tall vehicles have collided with it over the years.
(Reproduced with kind permission of John Cannon)

A WIDE AND busy new road (Park Way) has appeared on the left of picture above – an extension of the Albion Way inner bypass. This is an area of town made uncomfortable by the need to accommodate the car. However, the relative peace of pedestrianised areas is only a few strides away.

THE QUEEN'S HEAD

QUEEN STREET IS an extension of East Street beyond the railway bridge. Many old postcard views show gala parades outside the Queen's Head, which suggests that it was a popular starting point for processions around the town. *(Reproduced with kind permission of John Cannon)*

CLIMATE CHANGE MAY have helped, but any self-respecting pub expects to cater for outside eating these days. The advertisement on the green awning shows continuity: King & Barnes has gone but its beers are now brewed in Dorset by Hall & Woodhouse, who bought and closed the Horsham brewery.

QUEEN STREET,
LOOKING EAST

THE OLD PHOTOGRAPH on the left was taken in about 1923, when the road surface was sufficiently uneven to allow a cyclist to find a parking place well away from the pavement. The hanging sign on the left advertises the Alexandra Inn.
(Reproduced with kind permission of John Cannon)

LITTLE HAS CHANGED architecturally, but, as can be seen in the modern photgraph above, the road is no place for cyclists today. The Alexandra Hotel's berth has been taken by the education franchise Kip McGrath, with – a sign of the times perhaps – a debt advice service operating on the floor above.

NEW STREET

THIS PICTURE ON the left dates from 1959 when the Gardeners Arms stood just a little up the road from Queen Street. Car ownership was still chiefly restricted to the well-to-do, and parking restrictions were completely unnecessary.
(Reproduced with kind permission of Cecil Cramp)

THE PUB HAS gone but it's good to see it remembered in the name of one of the many new developments at this end of the road. The street was previously known as Pest House Lane after the institution of around 1725 where people with contagious diseases were sent. It was renamed around 1830, perhaps to appease local sensibilities.

POTTER'S CORNER

THIS IS WHERE Springfield Road, off to the right, meets London Road. In this 1950s view (right) there is a garage a little way along London Road under an Austin Cars sign.
(Reproduced with kind permission of Cecil Cramp)

TODAY THE CORNER site is home to a strange-looking building, which houses

flats above a lighting shop. London Road continues for a few hundred yards before coming to a dead-end at Albion Way.

LONDON ROAD

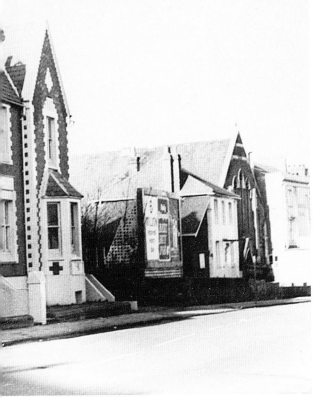

A VIEW OF London Road looking north, with the Methodist church in the background (left). The first church here opened in 1832, but within fifty years the congregation had outgrown the building and this new one was erected on the site, using bricks, tiles and pews from its predecessor.
(Reproduced with kind permission of John Cannon)

THE CHURCH IS still there today but Albion Way and a single large building have replaced everything in the foreground of the earlier picture. An underpass leads to the pedestrianised Medwin Walk, named after Thomas Medwin, a local solicitor. One of his sons, also called Thomas, was a friend of the poet Shelley and wrote his biography.

WORTHING ROAD

THIS PHOTOGRAPH OF around 1950 (left) looks north towards the centre, a road sign directing drivers to the main routes out of town. Before the days of bypasses you would follow the Worthing Road north through the centre of Horsham on the way to Dorking and eventually to Clapham Junction in South London.
(Reproduced with kind permission of John Cannon)

THIS IS NO longer a major thoroughfare and there have been other changes too – although the two houses in the centre of the older picture can still be glimpsed through the trees. On the right of the modern photograph above, two of Horsham's more recent developments can be seen, including its airy, plate-glass bus station.

Other titles published by The History Press

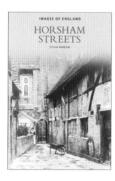

Horsham Streets

SYLVIA BARLOW

A thriving and bustling market town, Horsham is a place with a sense of its own identity. From its early origins it has been well known for its sheep, cattle and corn markets. *Horsham Streets* commemorates the people who lived there, their occupations and events taking place in the town in earlier centuries and shows how national events have influenced its development. Illustrated with over 100 evocative photographs and ephemera, this absorbing book captures Horsham's heritage and offers a unique glimpse into the town's past.

978 0 7524 4305 8

Horsham's Independent Bus Services

LAURIE JAMES

Horsham's Independent Bus Services looks at the varied bus companies that once served the Sussex market town of Horsham from the turn of the twentieth century to the present day.

Laurie James tells of the ups and downs of the humble companies that operate bus services in and around Horsham. Profusely illustrated with many images, the book will be of interest to both locals and bus enthusiasts alike.

978 0 7524 4441 3

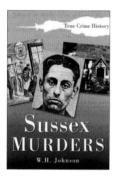

Sussex Murders

W. H. JOHNSON

Contained in this book are the stories behind some of the most notorious murders in Sussex's history. Among the gruesome cases featured here are the chief constable who was bludgeoned to death in his own police station, the gang of smugglers who tortured and buried one of their two victims alive, and the waiter who danced away the days while his lady friend's body lay mouldering in a trunk in his lodgings. This book is a must-read for crime enthusiasts everywhere

978 0 7509 4127 3

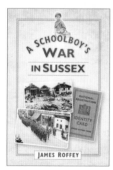

A Schoolboy's War in Sussex

JAMES ROFFEY

Although only children at the time, the Second World War had a permanent effect on the schoolboys who lived through the conflict. Watching a country preparing for war and then being immersed in the horrors of the Blitz brought encounters and events that some will never forget. Now in their seventies and eighties, many are revisiting their memories of this period of upheaval and strife for the first time. Due to it proximity to the south coast, West Sussex was a dangerous place in the wartime years, and this poignant book documents events indelibly inscribed on a generation's minds.

978 0 7524 5518 1

Visit our website and discover thousands of other History Press books.

www.thehistorypress.co.uk